Singing Back the Darkness

Other Books by KP Liles

Spring Hunger, Plain View Press, 2008

Singing Back the Darkness

KP Liles

Books™

The New York Quarterly Foundation, Inc.
New York, New York

NYQ Books™ is an imprint of The New York Quarterly Foundation, Inc.

The New York Quarterly Foundation, Inc.
P. O. Box 2015
Old Chelsea Station
New York, NY 10113

www.nyqbooks.org

Copyright © 2012 by KP Liles

All rights reserved. No part of this book may be used or reproduced in any manner whatsoever without written permission of the author except in the case of brief quotations embodied in critical articles and reviews.

First Edition

Set in New Baskerville

Layout and Design by Raymond P. Hammond

Cover Photo: "Alaska on Edge #9" by Dennis Lind Beery | www.dennislind.com

"The Muse" (p. 85) appears courtesy of Dennis Lind Beery

Author Photo: ©Molly DeKruif | www.theblinkofaneye.com

Library of Congress Control Number: 2012941099

ISBN: 978-1-935520-66-5

Singing Back the Darkness

Acknowledgments

"Palin Country" and "'Later, Jim" first appeared in *The New York Quarterly*.

"Listening to Arctic Thunder" first appeared in *ICE-FLOE*.

"25th Anniversary" aired on Alaska Public Radio's weekend show, AK.

"A Long Way from Cape Town" first appeared in *Stoneboat*.

Abundant thanks to all the kind, hard-working souls behind these literary outlets for their respectful handling of my work. And for their impeccable taste.

I'd like to express my gratitude to Marian Call and Jeannie Rose Field. For the stage time given to me, yes, but mostly for their truly life-saving support.

"Studio Harbor" I dedicate to Erin Pollock and Steph Kese.

"Healed" was written for Mom and Mark.

"My friend, by now you've made your way" exists (the same might be said for all of my poems) thanks to the friendship and guidance of Matthew Gavin Frank.

for my family—

*Mom, Dad, Diadette, Mark,
Paul, Courtney, and Annalise*

Contents

Singing Back the Darkness / 15
What a Wonderful World / 19
Palin Country / 20
After Watching *Eternal Sunshine of the Spotless Mind* / 22
"Later, Jim" / 24
Chase / 26
Bright Bleak Hope / 28
Plight Simulator / 33
Camouflage / 34
Listening to Arctic Thunder / 36
Iraq Lament / 37
The War Phallus / 39
Mind on Trial / 40
Cojones Meditation / 45
Wart / 49
Adolescent Song / 51
Bully / 53
Attend My Ten Year High School Reunion? / 55
Why I Hate Kids / 56
Tiggy / 61
Dissolution / 63
Expletive Song / 65
The Midday Voice of George Yeats / 67
25th Anniversary / 69
The Door There Is Devastation / 71
Divorce Blues / 73
Studio Harbor / 77
Too Many Places / 79
Healed / 81
Switch / 83
You Are, Are You? / 88
Appreciation / 89

Froot Loop Infinity and Beyond / *91*
A Long Way from Cape Town / *95*
Poems without Headlines / *98*
Holy Love / *99*
Dinner Party / *101*
…because / *103*
The Pain of Divorce / *106*
My friend, by now you've made your way / *111*

The people dreamed and fought and slept as much as ever. And by habit they shortened their thoughts so that they would not wander out into the darkness beyond tomorrow.

—Carson McCullers, *The Heart Is a Lonely Hunter*

Our heart wanders lost in the dark woods.
Our dream wrestles in the castle of doubt.
But there's music in us.

—Jack Gilbert, "Horses at Midnight Without a Moon"

Singing Back the Darkness

It can't
resurrect the dead, can't
reprieve the spouse
alternating beds.

Let's not pretend it inspires
soldiers to put down guns,
makes thieves decent
or leaders just.

It can't compare with the succor
of drink, a full stomach, or
the childish genius of kissing.

Let's not confuse it with
hope.

A companion that offers
no friendship, no future,
that will likely restart
the enervated battery of memory.

Stranded on a street
of cardboard-housed dreams
and barrel-burnt desires,

all singing
back the darkness can do is say:

I know you.

Your snoring, ravenous mouth
will devour me,
but now

I have eyes, words,
and the breath to lift them

                              to the face

in the church bathroom mirror.

What a Wonderful World

Doves were at war. Wingless angels prowled the streets with billy clubs and jacked cars for kicks. I didn't mind. I drank wine with breakfast while enjoying the standup routine of a comic lacking any semblance of self-confidence. Infants lined the bar, and there was a nursery for adults. I owned a gorgeous house without walls and lived uncomfortably in a time without passing. An empty Trojan horse forced me from my kingdom and into the desert where I wandered eons with a bear that didn't hibernate. Plants grew in darkness. People fought by kissing, made truces by murder. Everyone searched frantically for a happiness called Pain and proved amazingly generous with greed. I achieved fitness in stillness, learned to calm my mind into a rage. I accepted a fate with choices and accumulated inattentive disciples. A childhood without imagination occupied my memory and somehow I became trapped in a casino that forbid betting, run by burka-clad hookers. I hardly need to say that when my eyes opened I couldn't tell if I was awake or dreaming, but, get this—when I showed up for work, I began weeping uncontrollably, and for the life of me I had no clue if I was in store for a tragic victory or a marvelous defeat.

Palin Country

Papers? Crossing this border
        requires proof
                of pure ambition.
If the guard senses any
        self-doubt or breathes
                a whiff of weakness,
all his life he's craved excuse
        to unload hate.
                If you expect work,
train your wolf-brain to follow
        the pack, say *Yes*
                Ma'am or stay silent;
it's best to blend in with snow
        and keep in mind
                aerial killings
are still sanctioned. Wildlife
        is big business—
                habitat equals
vast natural resources.
        If you dizzy
                when troubled, run. Don't
look back until you've made it
        to Long Island.
                If you laugh at jokes
about seeing Russia, you're
        guaranteed pain.
                Be sure spouses smile
and that your children exude
        camera charm—
                it's the only way
to survive. This is no place
        for family.
                Hold tight to your faith

while hucksters preach religion
      sold on Main Street.
           Embrace the absurd.
Pack for a long cold season
      of dark scrutiny.
           Celebrity
will buy safe passage for a time,
      but novelty
           fades. When that happens,
pray you can trade office for
      personal gain.
           Go rogue. Shelve values,
ditch courage, deny loyalty.
      Hide your heart.
           It can't save you here.

After Watching *Eternal Sunshine of the Spotless Mind*

I take back all the times I wished myself dead—
the day after my wife left and I couldn't
rise from bed, August 15th 2001
three a.m. Carl sobbing into the phone
Stage 5, John's fourth grade roller skating party
walking past laughing friends after
painting the bathroom with urine,
that afternoon flight around my 23rd birthday
when the houses of my hometown looked aligned
like headstones. The grill lid barely down
over barbecue ribs and Jesse
blurting *I'm pregnant…*
How I tried to eat my pantry bare of shame,
feed my defeats to forgetfulness,
but these shelves replenish themselves so while
I'm gorging on lowest moments I might
as well take stock of my prize shortcomings:
mocking Brian's stutter in high school,
cheating on Irene, and stealing ten bucks
from the till at Chevron every shift
for two years. I'm not searching for forgiveness
or fool enough to believe that saving
my past will make me a better man. No,
the name of this game is self-preservation
*and it sure would be a lot easier
if I were fighting to hold onto Kate Winslet.*
I am the slow-learning child still grasping
at the lesson: what you run from will haunt you,
what you try to erase will brighten your hell.
Memory, I grab you by the wrist
and drag you back into the hospital
to stare at grandpa's stroke-wilted face
and to say the goodbye you never gave.
I force your hand to re-feed the Portmans'

basset hound chocolate. I strap your
drunken vision behind the wheel of Mona's
Jaguar and re-launch over the guard rail.
Mind, I'm buying a lifetime's worth of tickets
to your funhouse, your mirrors. I will relish
the pain reflecting from all angles and
keep my eyes open to the awful truth
I've avoided all my days—somehow
everything alive here is meant for this world.

"Later, Jim"

He's heard it 20, 30 times,
Tim a little more lit than usual
promising, "I'm gone, out of this place—
this shitty life—for good,"
and he pours one for the road
because he knows his regulars
like the outcome of the Cubs' season,
toll booths, his sister's
over-salted but otherwise delicious
Thanksgiving dinner.

The bar towel wipes away
fingerprints and the damp rings
of each knocked-back dream.
Some nights he wonders if his job
is to kill or to feed yearning,
then thinks *Jesus, Jim,*
slugs a shot of Crown and stacks
the glasses hot from the dishwasher.

Each night he follows
work gripes, talk of home lives
slapping around the bar
faster than a hockey puck,
and he likes them all
(except those who bring in their fights)—
lovers who come together or split,
the ones who only speak hello,
their drink, and thank you,
Chuck ramping onto his stool
like a Porsche into V.I.P. parking,
everyone who cheers or boos the team.

The door closes behind Tim,
but the air remains disturbed
with the sound of his goodbye,
his oath, "for good."
Jeers from the pool table, a request
for jukebox quarters.
Thank God Journey's End.
The ballgame over, music
riffs into familiar rock lullaby,
bottles clang like church bells.
Jim pours the last draft of last call,
resumes cleaning, eases everything
back where it belongs,
beginning to taste the cigarette
he'll light as he locks up
and prays that tomorrow
he'll quit this scene and never return.

Chase

Saved from the back of the amusement park
chute leading to the tellers, I feel
the curses of the Latino and black
customers cook my pale skin
the fiery pink of lechón or chitlins.
Hot, tired, I'm led down a white hallway
by a blue-suited, cherub-cheeked young man
into his blue and white office, where he
processes my paycheck, bumping my net worth
from $8.67
to digits that barely cover bills and rent.
Still, this week, a cold sixer in the fridge.
"You know," he says—this I've been prescreened for—
"we have a promotional interest rate
right now for new savings accounts opened
with a minimum balance of twenty-
five thousand dollars." I wait like the calf
in the slaughterhouse for laughter, from him,
from me, from the hidden cameramen
filming this mockery of my finances,
but he's not joking, so I try to figure
how many iced teas I would have to pour
while reciting the daily specials
to pay down my debts then have an extra
twenty-five grand to pass between banks
as if playing frisbee in the park;
how many corporate board meetings
I would need to crash, machete in hand,
to eliminate all prickhead questions
from any routine transaction; how many
white bankers would need to be imprisoned
to earn fiscal sense and security
for the average American worker...
"Hmm," I nod my head. "Let me think about it."

Blood, a pitch-forked mob at my eyes' gate.
And I'll take my twenty bucks for groceries
in rolls of pennies, please, in a tube sock.
Let me deposit a little clarity
back into your bank's name. Let me transfer
the only color absent in your
institution's interior design.

Bright Bleak Hope

If you think hope is a white sand beach,
you probably have sun poisoning
and require medical attention, or

you've been swimming against the tide
for hours and gone five feet from your towel.

I know, I know, the sand is so soft,
the beer bottles sweat—OH, so cold. Hope feels
like the last affordable vacation.

Hope is the derelict building
you must flee immediately.
Hope is that daily bowl of ice cream,

eyes averted from the scale's truth.
(Who said poetry shouldn't hurt?)
I hate to bear the bad news,

but your grip is slipping
and there's no net beneath you:

while you wait for lotto results,
God, your children to come to the rescue,
whole crops of opportunity wilt;

someone will patent your invention,
develop your brilliant script;
the greedy will continue to wreck

everything good in the world—
all the best land, decent wages,
movies, food, skylines, live concerts,
pensions and educations—

happily investing your future
in lucrative warfare—

they will never tire of adding
more disparity and fear.

Which isn't to say you should despair.

Hope is the shrewd teacher who
withholds reward to spur the best in you.

Hope, a lean, champion dancer,
demands your feet move first.
Hope is a vicious sparring partner.

How many more broken noses
will you suffer before you learn
to raise those gloves eye-level?

Make hope your most aggressive word,
the coin that lights fire.
Hold your fists high, man! Fight like hell.

Plight Simulator

(found poem)

Things should not be like this.
Something has gone wrong somewhere.
To live like this, surrounded by trash—
are we animals? Look at this village!
Flies are the only things that thrive here.

Finally! Someone to take care
of this terrible situation.

You have no manners, American.
> *What does it matter?*

Times were good here, but outsiders
have destroyed everything.
> *The days of our glory are long ago.*

Many are falling ill or starving. Please help them.
> *The only thing our government*
> *knows how to do is squabble*
> *and fight like roosters.*

You can give us protection
and stop making empty promises.
Do I look like a terrorist? I am
an ordinary person.
> *Squabble and fight like roosters,*
> *the only thing*
> *our government knows how to…*

If you're not going to help us, you should go.
> *The days of our glory are long ago.*

Please leave before someone sees us talking.
> *What does it matter?*

Don't ask me anything else.

There is nothing to tell.

Camouflage

Grim green,
snow white,

every fairy tale
shade in the books.

Each desert's sands,
all the cityscapes,

the woods, a cold
slaggy sea—

easy matches
for a military

crayon box.
So many hues to use.

There's a perfect disguise
for any lie. A soldier

will bury
in any terrain.

But one color
no army can cover.

For that to happen,
we'd have to battle

on lava, or Mars,
fight while burning.

Coat a man
in blood. Issue him

a uniform
of fire. He should be

well-suited
for war.

Listening to Arctic Thunder

(Elmendorf Air Show Song)

As planes streak overhead, yes,
patriotism thrills the blood.
My heart beats quicker
to the thought of distant widows wailing,
buildings obliterated,
men reading their local papers
fleeing in terror.
                    Who could have imagined
oil prices would climb so high
at such great speed! Who could've envisioned
the goodwill of the world
nose-diving
with such exemplary dexterity!

So exciting
one forgets vanishing pensions,
inadequate health care,
untenable debts. O my, how
those bluebirds make the spirits soar,
pride swell, the mind swoon
with dreams of all human
ingenuity serving
the perpetual war machine.

God bless the Angels.
Let fear ring. May the
sky never quiet.

Iraq Lament

Sixty-two dead from a suicide bomb...

In my well-lit room, cup of ginseng tea...
Seeing the number in print incinerates
my good mood then chills my wits...

as if, in the perfect rows of letters,
I were staring into a case
of refrigerated news...
                          as if the dead
are no more than sad slabs of meat...

What can I find in these daily reports
other than the cold certainty
that I am a stranger to the U.S.-
(my homeland!) steeped madness
of Iraqi streets...

                 checkpoints, crackdowns,
gun battles, beheadings and torture,
sectarian slaughter, the earth
sown with roadside bombs...

the endless harvest of hate...

What can any one man removed
or at the center of this violence...
Have we learned, after centuries
of evolution, how to crawl
out of the muck and stand upright
only to behave...

Suppose the human brain is more than
an atavistic survival machine,
each mind a flesh-shaded lamp of intellect;

perhaps the time approaches us when
only the vigil of small reading lights
saves our cities from the primal dark...

The War Phallus

Mushrooms, pummels, burns up
jungles and villages, erupts
in city centers, explodes in
every desert cave. There's not a
more well-traveled whore.

On the home front, certainly the
happiest cock on the block—
each family room glows with
the light of the tube, the erotica
of violent movies, serial
dramas, and the evening news.

Loving to harden enemies,
stroked daily by despots,
elected leaders, contractors, and
legislators—left handed,
right handed—
the War Phallus salutes
army grunts and generals,
women, men, terrorists
and peace-keeping killers alike.

Sheathed in national security
to ensure endless
safe sex for the Head
of State, nothing's better than this:
it   O, God   crawling closer, so
eager, out of its mind—
watching democracy as it goes down
O, Yes   goes down, goes down.

Mind on Trial

When I am brought before
the high court
this will be my sworn testimony

I knowingly did my best
to slaughter
fear

I behaved
like a genocidal madman
when warring against
millions of insecurities

In the ring with the grand champion
Aggression
as the bell rang rang rang
I kept up
a savage calm-beating

I can already see
the jurors' astonishment
and hear the appalled masses wondering
How could he be
so cold-blooded
therefore
I will confess

It was easy
A true heart
and a still mind
will slay any self-loathing
I've no wish to escape conviction
and I offer no apology
I beg you

let me begin now
serving my time

Ten consecutive life sentences
of peace

Cojones Meditation

Driving home from yoga class
still energized, relaxed—almost amused
by a radio rant on the global
economic meltdown—I am
stopped at a red light
directly eye-level with a pair
of enormous, blue rubber testicles
dangling from the bumper of a pickup truck.

First, I scan the sky for confirmation
of the planet's imminent destruction. Then I look
for another witness with whom I might share
a nod, a *Can you believe this jackass?*
But it seems I am left to take measure
of this Dodge Ram's synthetic reproductive parts
alone. *If cars can now procreate*
surely we can devise a way to lower the cost
of gasoline. Now that's what I call a hybrid!
Blue? Really? Not very manly—
was it the Volvo or the Mercedes that left this
poor metal hunk in a lurch?

I know the road to enlightenment,
on which I try to remain
an earnest traveler, would have me overlook
or look through this display of the ego's madness.
I would not scoff at the driver's identification
with his truck or his need to gender steel.
I would experience neither rage, contempt,
nor separateness from my brother. But so
much of me wants to call my friends
who first reported seeing this vehicle
and tell them *You weren't lying.*
I'm idling in traffic behind this cretin

deafening himself with bass, who's compensated for
his scrawny crushed nutsack
by affixing rubber balls to the bumper
of his truck. Balls on his truck!
What good are peace and balance if I can't
die laughing at the outrageous stupidity
of machismo? Must I embrace this moron
as an equal if I am to free my soul?
So many miles to go. So many miles.

I imagine us swapping vehicles and lives—
me speeding off to a rally of highway
abominations, deciding if I should park beside
the Impala with spinning hubcaps, the Subaru
whose license plate is festooned with lights
and ticker messaging, or the van with flipping
advertisement panels; my odd companion
venturing to the yoga studio,
surrounded by women of all ages
in leotards, the only man in the room,
awakened during the kind of inward looking
I myself have forbidden.

Not fair
I hear myself whine, which only
makes my anger floor it
as my mind tries to shift
into the calming practices with all the skill
of a teenager murdering the clutch.
Ordinarily, I am contented
with the world's turns, pleased
to pass time tuning up tiny verses
of dreams, questions, prayers,
sending them on their way

with the same quiet love
and duty that I find in replenishing
my kitten's bowl each morning.
Sometimes the wheels fly off.
Happiness disappears like savings accounts
emptied by whispers in the market.
What kind of man are you? What does it mean
to be a man these days?

To have moved beyond the indignity
of the gym locker room, the awkwardness
of a shaving lesson, or the suggestion
that it might be time to consider using
deodorant, and, of course,
the earth-blooming relief
of the first girl fumbling with my fly—
to have scraped together some loose change
of experience into something resembling
the currency of manhood
only to discover Shiva snickering
at the intersection, "So, you think you've grown
into an adult male of superior intellect,
kindness, and strength, nearing grace?
Well, congratulations. Would you
like some insight as a gift? Here—
balls in your eye, kid."

                      I don't know
where to go with this, and I have no choice
but to keep driving when the light turns green
and the *cojones azules* swing
down a street different from the one
I must take.   Spared from locking eyes

with a man perhaps too at ease
with letting it all hang out,
I continue home, comforted and strangely
saddened by a conviction that,
squeezed into his truck's cab,
he, too, is scratching at something
more cumbersome and hairier
than he can hope to understand.

Wart

In my fourteenth year, in the mound of my thumb,
war came to my body. For an entire month
I watched the horseshoe skin battlements build up,
thicken while thwarting the attacks of my fingers,
and dared sound no alarm in fear
the loathsome mark might hasten my doom.
How could I explain to my parents
the ruin I'd brought upon our house?
Afternoons spent sliding and fighting in mud?
Stolen Slurpies from the convenience store?
All that homework time wasted taking measure
of the advancing front of Chelsea's sweater?

I scrubbed and scrubbed but still
the unnatural tectonic uplift
continued—and the crater pooled
with an ineffaceable glaucous scum—
until one morning, unable to touch
a bowl of Cheerios, my mother
discovered *it* and rushed me to the doctor
who named my curse: verruca vulgaris.
Then he prescribed his horrific remedy:
No baseball the rest of the summer.
No bat handling of any kind.

Deprived of my favorite pastimes,
what could I do? I shunned the outdoors
and tried to hide myself in books—
*The Lord of the Rings, Prince Caspian,
The Sword of Shannara.* I camped
in fantasy, in the company of monsters,
searching for a spell that would make shame
vanish forever. But each story's magic failed.

Nothing could sway my attention away
from the waxy cauldron on my palm.

The wart boiled with red and black dots.
I had had enough. Left in the car,
my mother mired in the post office,
rank with hate, I snatched a pen off the floor
then dug into the lumpy bog and
shoveled out a putrid truffle.
I waited for gushing slime and blood
but there was only a slight tingle
as I felt the life go out of it. Free!

Or so I thought. But to this day,
whenever embarrassment scrapes
over my skin like a muffler
dragging across the street, I look
down at my burning hand, expecting sparks.
I stare into the strange white crescent
seared in my flesh and wonder if my heart, too,
might master that same dark art of the pen
to transform any ugliness
into a luminous, beautiful scar.

Adolescent Song

Break the rules, burn the churches
to clear room for grasshoppers—
raze all claims upon your life.
No. If your nerves seethe desire
to core the world's rotten order,
lead a life free of violence—
nurture quirks, unbending calm,
let laughter sing your genius,
then kayak through Alaska.
If you insist on truth,
listen to your own breathing.
Drown dolts in oceans of silence.
Do your best to harm no one
while your identity teethes,
though it would be easier
to eat knives. When the rich kids
would have you envy their cars,
marvel at their plastic lives,
hand them a library card
and a jar of fireflies.
Piss hard on their door handles.
Joke, paint when ordered to speak.
Feast on hope and drink the wind.
Curiosity is the
only school worth attending.
For fuck's sake run barefoot
in a field. Shun shopping malls.
Harvest joy and tears like wine.
Make music. And disbelieve
in heroes. When love base jumps
down your spinal cord, open
your heart like a parachute.
I wish things were otherwise—
the world is full of soul-sick

shysters desperate to
smear your spirit as a salve
for their decay. Love them.
Love everyone—let love tear
with jailbreak madness around
your veins. Let your love parade
engulf and crazy the streets.
Somewhere hot gooey cookies,
lava cools to build new earth.
Fear not the loud anguished ghosts
of your parents' defeat.
Above all, you must forget
the gibberish of older
men like me. Aye, to go
another round with what I
know now. That useless lament.
Forgive my late pilgrimage
to rebellion's black altar:
may we all dare to live like
courageous youths as we age.

Bully

He rumble-barrels up the bus steps
like a football team charging
out the tunnel into the lighted stadium—
pure, electrified punishment—
and slams himself up against
the window, the artillery of Metallica
guitar riffs firing from
headphones through his head,
through the air, annihilating the sounds
of friends talking, homework swapping,
flirting.

       His school day starts
in detention, in the silence where
he can almost hear the boyfriend's bruises
smoldering in his flesh and his rage
meditates to his mother's mantra *fucking loser.*
Scorn adopts him and begins to teach
his manhood, coaches him to punch
the dickhead Craig who took his
starting quarterback role,
stub out cigarettes on the hoods of cars,
screw Leslie or Tammy or
anyone who will accept the tall
unsheathed cord of his body.

His teachers fear and resent him too much
to try to convince him that Mark Twain,
math, Einstein, history, might be
talismans to fight his pain.
A counselor's ignorant sincerity,
asking him *Why are you so angry? Why
do you think you crave negative attention?*
arms his hate and triggers his spite.

He hits the hallways hungry,
rushes into the cafeteria where
Tyler the dentist's son sits,
lucky enough to have a full tray,
untorn clothes, unlucky enough
to have risked the side-long glance
seen through the steel shaft
of the bully's vision, and unlucky enough
for him to have found the answer to
each kid's question *Why me?*
Because everybody pays,
everybody pays through the teeth.

Attend My Ten Year High School Reunion?

      Does the butterfly
                          fly
           back inside
      the chrysalis
to again crawl as a caterpillar?

Why I Hate Kids

Griefs: those sullen brats.
Truly the most hideous children.

Attend to their needs, give in,
and they scream, "I hate you!"

Spoiled pets, ignorant woefully
of the world beyond themselves—

immune to discipline. Unteachable.
Have you watched these crying demons

cling to a parent's leg in the park
like deranged koala bears?

My God they've grown fat,
gorging on high-fructose suffering

while cement-faced to the suggestion
of fresh air or exercise.

Devious, nasty creatures
that remember each long-ago mistake

and all your failed promises.
Say goodbye to your hair and sleep

when they approach drinking age.
Vasectomy…Hysterectomy, anyone?

Let's not fool ourselves into thinking
abstinence will empty our cribs.

As the candles burn down
and night deepens,

before we whirl into bed together
like sagging fighters at the end

of a savage bout, let us first undress
our agonies under the encouraging moon

(that second bottle of wine unopened)
and stop making these babies!

Tiggy

You can't find a friendlier cat.
Every stranger she greets
with a little hello yelp
and Fosbury Flop into a lap.
Scratch behind her ear or under
her chin and her purr engine
hums along like a Bentley.
Such ease with people. If human,
this would be called resilience
or forgiveness, given her start—
declawed, left defenseless against
three rough Boxers, before that found
eating in a dumpster and seen
flicked from a speeding car's window
like a cigarette.   It takes such
small effort to care for
the least among us. Two scoops
of dry food, bedside water glass,
a morning handful of tuna-
flavored treats and her scraggly
dun-colored coat smoothed and softened.
Her eyes cleared into dime-bright-pools.
Part tiger, part feline Buddha—
somehow her dignity survived
abandonment. Pure cat genius.
Too bad we're not consanguineous.

When my wife left me then divorced,
flattened, without will to live,
Tiggy would sit on my chest or
simply near me on the bed,
depending on how hard I wept,
prayer-light on her toothless paws.

I'm not sure whose character showed—
whose wildness burnished more.

Food gone to dust. Eyes damned with fear.
No claws to fight back the brutal
sadness and hatred.
                        Outcast
into a loveless world,
roaming the deep shadows of grief,
Tiggy's company saved me
from madness. From the mean streets
of self-loathing. From starving my heart.
I'd look into her eyes and trust
that maybe with one night's sleep,
a few bites to eat, maybe,
if I stayed open to kindness,
then maybe tomorrow I might
leave bed and go to the window
ready to face a milk-white day.

Dissolution

Not only a solvent for marriage
but, if you're not careful, life as well.
An odd word meaning an agreed upon
or amicable divorce. It achieves
the same violence, begins eating
the supposedly unbreakable bonds
from the moment those horrifying words
are first spoken: *This isn't what I want;*
I'm so sorry, but I've made a mistake;
I love you, but I'm not in love—
take your pick, or collect your misery
for hearing this perfect trifecta.
The gavel drops quickly in court,
but the work in the body goes slow.
Some days a fiery agony—a million
scalding hooks weighted with lead
tug beneath the skin. Some days
the air is anesthetic, the mind
a house of impervious numbness
not even the ghosts of sleep
or hunger can enter. Always,
Time is the soundless fuse
promising the explosion
that will rip you apart along
the countless seams of your anxiety.
Cigarettes and whiskey befriend you
by adding variety to pain. O, but nothing
can dissolve the night, the perpetual fact
of the empty bed, the nightmares—
arguments had, arguments imagined,
the cheating envisioned
with exquisite detail. Each new thought
a shiny coin tossed into the overflowing fountain
of hateful wishes. My personal favorite terror—

her black mare stomping me,
its nostrils flaring before my closing eyes,
hot breath on my face as I die
and wake to a migraine, which reminds me
I alone must find a way to heal
or this suffering will kill.

Expletive Song

O, how I laughed. George Carlin
questioning the audience
if anyone knew what his brown ribbon
stood for: "Eat shit, motherfucker! Eat shit,
motherfucker!" And, O, how many days
before shuffling out the door
to greet my insane neighbors head on
I've dressed my spirit in a brown suit.
Two months running now I've done so
in anticipation of bumping into the rich
sonofabitch who seduced my wife,
readied myself à la
Inigo Montoya in *The Princess Bride*,
"…You killed my father. Prepare to die."—
Listen, you soulless cocksucker. No matter
how many wives you purchase
or mansions you build, no matter how many
wads of cash you stuff
into the hole in your heart, you will
never fill your emptiness. And good luck
with my gold digger-whore of a wife.
You two make a beautiful couple.
O, how cursing sings through the veins—
eyes harden into volcanic glass
the blood a torrent of alertness
pleasure dancing like a sparkler
at the base of the brain. How else
to cope with the goddamn indignity
of our humanity? How else to survive
the bullshit mining our streets?
How else can we walk this earth
without malice and vengeance
wrecking our minds unless we center

firmly in our being, raise our fists
and summon all of our intelligence
into a joyful shout, "Fuck you, World!
You don't own me!"

The Midday Voice of George Yeats

Georgie?
> Who speaks through me now? I've heard no voices
> since my husband's death.

Georgie Hyde-Lees? Surely you remember me?
> That name. Is familiar, from my past.

We once talked with one another as easily
as the birds chirp, before you summoned
the other spirits for your new spouse...
> O, but he was so blue
> when we first married. I only meant to distract him,
> and I so loved him.

Yes, lucky girl, you "had the virtue
of being in love with him." How could anyone "forget
the wisdom that you brought, the comfort that you gave."
> How dare...Such sarcasm is uncalled for
> coming from an Old Acquaintance
> as I am a widow still spun by grief.

Please, you're no longer bound to the gyres and visions.
You may stop clucking like the "hen that picks up scraps."
> Your brash words betray your ignorance of me.
> I've been no unwitting puppet.
> I sought the occult. I joined the Golden Dawn. I
> controlled the pen during the automatic sessions.

And when you kept on past numb muscles and nerves?
When you demanded he leave you be, thinking only of verse?
> Proof we were guided by my volition.

When you said nothing of his affairs
because you knew how proud he was?
When, after years of matrimony,
he still posed questions to your Sybil
about Maude?
> I fully understood
> the medium of our love. I was a poet's wife—
> a bridge between confusion and peace, weakness

> *and action, theory and practice. I was the instrument of everything.*
> *I was! You know nothing.*

If you say so. But, did the Midnight Voice
that authored such greatness
once, Once, transmit your own concerns? Did it ever conduct
directly to you, or for you,
as I do now?

> *You know nothing. I have no faith in you.*

Georgie Hyde-Lees! Is it so difficult
for someone who speaks with ghosts
to hear herself?

25th Anniversary

Having whet his dread
of an exorbitant bill all week,
Charlie sulks in his chair
at the world famous restaurant
as a roasted rack of lamb—
the best meat he's ever eaten,
flown in from New Zealand, cooked
a perfect medium rare—
cools on the plate "for the dogs."
"A few more bites," she urges,
and he forks the fruit-laced couscous
around his plate like a horse's tail
scatters flies. His mind wed
to dissatisfaction for so long
it could foretell his next fifty years.
"Charles, look, the waiters fold
new napkins each time
someone goes to the bathroom."
With her knife, Laura assembles
tiny portions of morel risotto,
Copper River King Salmon,
and horseradish crème fraîche
like a pharmacist filling a prescription,
and remembers her husband
down on one knee, trembling,
so sweet, so sweet.
To her surprise, he agrees to dessert—
a chocolate ginger tart
with pear-caramel sauce
and praline ice cream—
which arrives, compliment of Chef,
candle-lit and topped
with a two-carat diamond ring.
"Charlie," Laura begins to cry.

"Chilled spoons." "They're trying
to numb my hands for the check,"
he cracks, cleaning the ring
of chocolate for his *lovely, silly girl*,
savoring the smallest of pleasures as if
her life depended on them.

The Door There Is Devastation

Having a husband
is the B to the O to the M to the B
my wife would tell her friends those
first months of our marriage when
her voice carried the lilt
of a hundred family and friends lifting
the dance floor, when her eyes shone as
delicious as our moonlit honeymoon dinners
and her smile reflected certitude in vows.
I laughed, too, joy
muting the spark, the hissing
five-month fuse of fidelity
already burning down. I laughed.
Detonation unthinkable—days of waking
to kisses, cats sharing the bed, bringing her
coffee as she readied for work
gone. Teeth chipped and ribs displaced
from sobbing, the fabled story of our love
turned elegy in a world stunned
cemetery gray, ears ringing with
D to the I to the V—as in
the division of assets—O to the R to the C—
as in demon-inhabited sleeplessness.
I laughed, the radar empty,
never having imagined that one day
I would reach for the final,
silent E like a phantom limb—
E as in freedom,
or in possibility—
that I would learn it is possible
to destroy a man's life utterly,
for a judge in Alaska to decree
his dream of permanence dead,
and for him to walk away

the very next day
along the shore of the Bay of Fundy
anew, better off,
wiser. Grief-wrung and ruined.
Almost unscathed.

Divorce Blues

Woke up this morning to a grave-dark dawn.
Woke up screaming into the grave-dark dawn
under a slab of air. My wife long gone.

At work, in dream, each meal, I see her face.
I go breathless each time I see her face.
She's made a mortuary of this place.

I feel nothing she said when our love died.
I feel nothing for you and our love died.
No, there's no one else, eyes nails as she lied.

Less than a year after our fateful day.
Over   a year after our fateful day
I smell honey—hydrangeas, her bouquet.

The young woman in white my wife. My wife!
God, stop her now from burying my life.

Studio Harbor

Paint glued into their hair, paint
caked on their hands and necks, glasses
flecked with plaster and paint,
their jeans a second skin of paint—
the walls swelling waves
of cast and colored faces—
no food or drink in sight,
the opening fast approaching—
a metal fan arguing with
the toxic air that had already
twice tried to kill them—
the two young women moved
throughout the cluttered studio
liked an aged couple dancing together
for thirty years—*"Do your friends
and lovers understand?"* I asked—
laughter—my God,
how bright those smiles at their work.
"Oh no, your suit." I looked down—
coming home from a wedding, the door
open, my own marriage four days away
from a court dissolution, I'd stopped in
to say hello, to bask in the company
of kind and self-possessed women,
to escape the night's dome of sadness
and its dreadful moon hanging
like an anvil—one splotch
of white oil paint on
the pant leg of my navy blue suit.
Over and over, I dabbed
the stain with a damp, greenish-
blackish bar of soap given to me
by the girls, smearing and thinning the paint
with waxy paper towels. For an hour.

So absorbed by the chore,
I could've been mistaken for a surgeon
trying to repair a heart.
Was it an artist's instructions
or the shadow of my unfaithful wife
casting her love for expensive clothing
that forced my hand? My fingers
satiny with paint. The suit
fused to my leg, slick as a seal's coat.
The fragrance of that one drop
impossibly thick, as rich
as the sea is deep—
enough to drown me in a world where
a flower can win a heart
or a song kill a man.
I dove into an ocean of paint.
For eight years I'd worked a job
I hated, paying the wife-spiked bills.
Eight years of words used
to sell, convince, promise, lie,
grease the menial wheels.
Eight years of words sinking
colorless to the floor.
      Never again.

Too Many Places

"...and at my funeral (your voice sparking
like the lit fuse of a bottle rocket),
I want Lynyrd Skynyrd's 'Free Bird' playing—
organs, orchestra, at least nine guitars..."
I picture your wife, losing at Rummy,
shaking her head; the picnic table jeweled
with beer bottle rings; your eyes reflecting
a packed stage, the earth shaking so violently
that every hawk, finch, dove or eagle
within twenty miles explodes from the trees
just as the singer cries "fly—high-igh,"
and the cannon fires your casket
into the Colorado, deep inside the Grand Canyon,
where your corpse will rock 'n' roll out to sea.
"Really?" I say. "I've always thought of you
as reserved, more of a Leonard Cohen
'Bird on a Wire' kind of guy—bare,
somewhat...repentant."
                        "Fuck that," you bellow
and—my peerless friend, for too long we've lived
worlds apart—you laugh into the phone so hard
my eardrum pounds in my throat and I'm nearly
deafened to time. O let me dream.
Then years separated would dull to hours.
Our lives might regain their everyday
a cappella luster. Dinner together
would mean grilled chicken and sangria
instead of a twelve course degustation
at Charlie Trotter's. Dog walks and campfires,
coaching our sons' baseball team, would out-burn
the feverish need for fellowship.
We'd no longer require the help
of art to sculpt every shared moment
into an unageing, perfect monument.

We'd play tennis as ourselves and not
as Federer and Nadal, the night sky
would enchant without the hand of Van Gogh,
you would not have to answer when Anton
Chigurh appears at your bedside and says
"Call it."
        I know, I know, my brother,
but can you blame me for jabbering on
when I know exactly what you will say
after you've recovered from laughing,
when I would forfeit all my desires
if I could prove you wrong or alter
your last words: "You will follow my instructions,
KP, and this bird you cannot change."

Healed

Look! How happy is our laundry
you're back in the yard
hanging it to dry—

the bedspread whirls
like Ginger Rogers' dress
leading on Astaire's legs.

Pillow cases, those
carefree sunbathers,
bask on winter holiday.

I can't fault our bedding
if its joy is retaliatory.
While you were gone,

I shied away,
cared nothing
for slow-baked blankets,

and prepared for the long sleep
of grief.
I used the machine.

Sun arches over the roof.
I shade my awe with glasses
as Thelonious would drop the lid

over his keys if he, too,
could watch your fingers pull
and place pins along the line.

When your mouth went slack
in the ambulance, your hand
ice in mine, I felt you die.

Our children's phone calls
hot-ironed my chest.
Who would remind me the rain

is *liquid sunshine,* or say
work, it's a four-lettered word?
Wait, what happened to goodbye?

That joke about no one
noticing you gone—

Above the linen horizon,
your closed-lip grin
restarts the world. Wind bells

a wheat-colored sheet around you.
And I see it:
you returned to the field

of our bed, under a gaping
harvest moon. I breathe
the chaff of your downy hair,

chaff of your kiss,
your tenderness, your sickness,
chaff of your tinny laugh.

For at least this one more night,
I swear I will love best
the parts of you first to go.

Switch

>(After Hanging *The Muse*)

Surely your stage-lit breast
is the microphone
amplifying the song of my kiss
and even the stadium's air
blushes after my lips.
O generous
instrument of pleasure, how
have we found ourselves
alone together? Head arched
over your scandalous shoulder,
hair and face indiscernible—
my blazing advocate of passion,
why have you kept
your eyes and mouth hidden?
You've been undone by bliss,
haven't you? Newly screwed
to my wall, the music
of fulfillment has ignited you
and your fire erupts
moonward. You are
woman's orgasm incarnate—
the neck-wrenched moaning,
night-splitting
hip-crazed O God O Yes coming
euphoria and fury
made paint.

>Did your
neon desire just flash brighter,
or...Oh,
I've been horribly mistaken.
Only pain fuels this burning.

One breast, half woman—
more corpse than curve.

How did I overlook
this mutilation?
Face nearly melted,
waist down already consumed
in a pyre, my innards recoil
from the glaze of necrophilia
now on my longing.
Your charring silhouette
sears my eyes. Tell me,
what record of wreckage
has the black box
stitched to your mouth preserved?
You were a student, dancing
your way through med school.
Abducted by your best customer,
forever haunting the club's pole.
You were an ordinary girl
embarrassed by your figure.
A wealthy suitor
tried to buy your "yes"
with his black Amex card,
and he murdered you
when he couldn't own your parts.
But, wait…

Your eyes *are* open
and in those tortured sockets
I see shock, treachery,
cool calculating spite.
                    Soulless spirit,
you are the minion of betrayal,

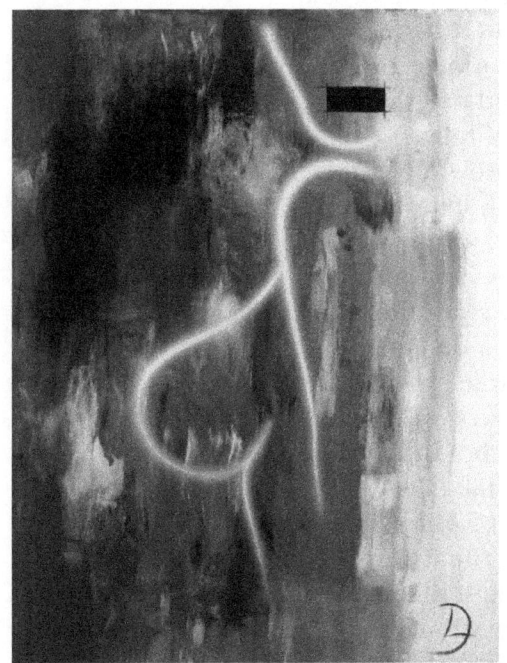
©Dennis Lind Beery

the ravaging angel of lust.
Now I recognize your background:
torched roses, faithless midnight.

O, how I've tried
to purge my palate of divorce,
to sing the oblivion of sex,
but you have canvased
my abandonment thoroughly
and colored my home
a theater of hurt.
Yes, I do know you. You've taken
her place, filled
the skeletal-white void of the wall.
I name you Coraline after
the nine o'clock film we'd agreed on
for our next date night,
the one projecting
from the dark screen on your face.
You hang above the very couch
where she faked
excitement for the latest vision
of our favorite dreamer Neil Gaiman.
Seen through the magic gemstone
of loss, everything is clear.
Did you think I'd forget
that odd tremor to her smile,
the unprovoked hostility that followed—
the mouth becoming a casket for joy?
Three days. And her frame
emptied of any love for me.
Or did you imagine
I'd think it coincidence
that you arrived the same day

she walked out the door for good
into her lover's BMW?
Did you, Coraline? My muse,
my torturer, dream girl
and dream eater.
You are the one
who embodies my sorrow.
You're the one who devours
fantasy. You teach me the art
of giving up finding
all that I've ever wanted
in this world.

You Are, Are You?

A paint stroke dashed ecstatically from God's brush.
The unexpected word—the lightning in a poem.

A bowl of steaming soup on a stormy winter day.
You are all of these, and you are none of them.

You are certainly not the owner of children,
your job, your country, the person your clothing

projects to the world, but you must be
the grace found in a stable yoga asana.

Trying to hold on to your essence
is like attempting to eat daylight.

How do you see yourself? Are you
a jumbo jet idling on the runway?

Applause at a concert? The newspaper
used to start a campfire? Are you the crimped flesh

and bared teeth or are you the smile? You are
a dam of worry or a river of laughter?

When you think of death, are you the lines of a hop-
scotch game or those chalked at the scene of a crime?

Don't answer, but tell me—are you the being
or are you only the life?

Appreciation

A frieze of chalk faces, top hats,
busts, cigars and martini glasses
runs along the bar's ceiling where the art
student, seated in the corner of his Parthenon,
sips a third over-tipped Cordon Bleu.
He half-stands to smooth his slacks and tug
his cardigan back in place—a boy
who's never tried on hope—as he waits for the server,
Sheri, for the shape of his name on her lips.
He thinks, *maybe these horn-rimmed specs...*

Like torch-uncovered figures in the caves of Lascaux,
young couples light then fade beyond
the tiny flames of votive candles. Men
arrive, pull off gloves, coats, scarves
like swords from scabbards. They cut into his view
of the jazz trio, start clapping for the bass, *as if
they're in on it, friendly with the band, have the right!*

The joint hasn't been the same (and Sheri agrees) since
going smoke-free last New Year's Eve.
The hazy, caramel glow behind the bottles,
now: an orange blasphemy. The new
sleek black bar-top, the walls
streaked a cool maroon—a bad Hopper.
Gone: Sheri's after-work cigarettes and her having him
describe the masterpieces he'd seen earlier,
her tired eyes widening briefly, and him imagining
their lives as paired lines of paint
illumining a giant canvas.

He turns to his right, ready to speak his piece
about the fundamentals at stake: light, color,
company. But the slumped absinthe drinker

and the rest of the Thursday night regulars
are nowhere to be found. Outside, Sheri
lights up and bolts for the running car
with the maître d' of Sacks Café behind the wheel.
Cognac whirls in his guts
like Pollock working out a nightmare.
He watches his sweaty hand smudge disappear
from the glass-topped table, then leaves, unnoticed,
from the place where he drew comfort from the cold.

Froot Loop Infinity and Beyond

I pour the remnants of cereal into the sink and watch the multi-colored milky wash whirl around the drain— marvel at the grainy galaxy and delight in having eaten stars for breakfast ; for three, maybe five seconds, heaven spins in the kitchen and I understand everything in the universe. And then I'm staring into the stainless steel oblivion of eternal wonder.

A Long Way from Cape Town

                        Ice-fog frosts
the bare-branched trees
      of Anchorage   into a vast
coral reef.
                My Mazda
                    swims the still mist
while Peter Mulvey and Anaïs Mitchell
 (an iPod live recording
         of a concert in Talkeetna, Alaska)
     sing about *The Book of Love*,
its unwieldiness,   its nonsense
 and brilliance   and the pleasure of sharing
              its sunken treasures
      again and again. And
         I'm so happily submerged
in this wintry Atlantis I am
         a little clownfish
   bright-eyed and so charming
            I deserve my own Pixar movie.
     Not really.   I look silly
        in orange
             and tend to dress only
   in shades of bruise.
I can barely swim
           and often leave the beach
 with ringing earaches; not to mention,
         my fondness of daydreams
would be hell on a director
    trying to call me out of the water,
       given my limited hearing,
  which probably explains why
     I'm driving on a road I don't recognize,
  the purpose for leaving home

long forgotten, or why my wife migrated
            to a different ocean.

                   I was saying something
        about orange or fish, wasn't I?
    Something about   love and music?
      I'm sure of it.   *My God,*
it's been eight months already.
I'm always thinking about the same damn things.
           Safeway?
                     Coffee! I was on my way
  to buy coffee, cream, and   and—dish soap.
              Sunlight blazing off ice.
                       Back to breathing air
         and boring bipedal chores—
            shopping, paying bills, grieving
                      and dodging despair.
   How odd to nearly drown
       midday,   dry,   no sight of sea.
                         O, but back home
                  I will take a walk,
        and glide down the streets
                    knifing the wind
  like the dorsal fin of a great white
                          patrolling to devour
anything—even forgiveness,   even rage—
         Or I will dip inside quietly   *Must be*
that long chapter "Loss and Heartbreak"
         makes The Book of Love so boring
    like the fluke of a sounding whale
                 as it cruises toward Hawaii.
  If anyone   sees me adrift
                           in my wandering
             or staring at

                    the sun's ripe rind
         like a damn fool, please remind me
      of which current   I was traveling—
                  I've always wanted to swim
                   in one of those huge shoals
                   of dancing fish,
                        wheeling in unison
                             through the dark deep.

Poems without Headlines

A phone rings and rings
        and the floorboards don't answer.
The ceiling's white glare.

Halloween, no plans.
I've only seen this one ghost.
        Jack o'lanterns smile.

        morning   no papers
on doorsteps   a city without
            obituary

            the cats zigzag crazed
      hairs raise   a painting missing
her shoe rack empty

Holy Love

Walking across a downtown park
alone on a Sunday afternoon...
a few sunbathers reading, barbecues...
the caroming shouts of children...
nearby church bells...
                    my senses nearly asleep
in the languorous summer heat
until I see two young lovers
beneath a tree laughing leaning
whispering kissing—O amorous ease!
How do they come by their bliss?
Do they fight for it every moment?
against everyone? against themselves?
Or do they accept it like rain,
the grass, the geese, the obvious
but once unbelievable
curvature of the earth...

As the bike path swerves me closer
the women break from their embrace
and busy themselves with lunch
and magazines...in fear of *me*?
Why...Perhaps they mistake me for
one of the dispersing congregation
newly inspired by scriptures,
which have been made into warrants
for slavery murder war
the brutal treatment of women...
Why wouldn't they assume I'm a threat
given the record of men's claims
as to what constitutes The Word?

I step heavily, troubled
that I'm somehow complicit

in stifling such scarce love,
and I try to imagine life
under the most severe code:
these lovers violate an order—
wouldn't they be dealt with
by the maker? Wouldn't kindness,
quiet belief in one's own creed,
better one's standing with God
more than fear, anger, judgment,
the fist of each individual
and imperfect righteousness?

I think of dark energy,
morels the year after a fire,
sea creatures on the ocean floor
—God manifest in infinite variety—
and I wonder, if God is Lord
of everything and everything is of
God's making, who can say these women
fall outside of God's design?
And why else deny them?
What's there to fear in their dreams
other than the reflection
of one's own love
not so purely given?

A sputtering kite whips like
flames in the slight wind, then crashes…
I look back—nothing changed.
Two women…left alone
to live freely, love freely…
Their eyes rise to mine, sharing a wish,
a felicity not otherwise found:
God grace me with the courage
to live as more Human than man.

Dinner Party

I can't say Diane surprised me when she tried
to curry favor with Quentin,

but, when Barbara asked for more
dry-rubbed pork,

I knew the wine had overflowed.
Or maybe Brian should shoulder the blame

for a few unexpected pairings—
insisting all the women have seconds

of his wild mushroom flan. Then again,
envy might have overcooked

my vision after years of my now
ex-wife pan-searing my

raw fear. Desire
has blackened many a jerked chicken.

More skeptic, traditional, than I would like
to admit, I have a hard time swallowing

variety as the spice of life.
Although, my nose tells me that

we are all poorly-trained cooks
likely to forget what we have

on the stove as we search for
the perfect marriage of ingredients.

"Pot Roast! Lasagna Bolognese!"
I hear the Grand Chef

shout as he clangs a spoon
against a giant pot

of boiling stock. "Season as you go,"
he reminds me, sensing my exhaustion

from the constant return of hunger.
"Imagination and curiosity is what

you want, is what you want,"
he says. Ah, the delicious sauciness of it all.

Careful with the salt, my friends.
Don't be so shy with the pepper.

...because

...because you wore my favorite color—
the rocks along the roadside red and sheer
...because the sudden shoots of your laughter
threw more oxygen into the car's air
...because sun's eager light ...because your legs
your snug skirt your red hair ...because music—
strange, fragile ...because, somehow, alone
with a woman the first time since disaster,
like the morning's sea I rolled easy calm
...because I imagined tasting your salt,
your lips surely cardamom flavored
...because your awkwardness, your candor
...because I'd offered you a heart of stone
and you were fine using me as a flint
...because I could not separate you
from the land the ocean spring's insistence
...because we were alive and felt neither
dirty nor endangered for it ...you were
the earth ...and because you could not know this
and because that day only you wore brown

...because the night, gracious coat-check,
asked for our clothes, color, our eyes,
histories, and gave us a ticket
we could exchange to reclaim them
...because Malbec-stained teeth ...because
candles, blood throbbing ...because
your hand running through my hair
...because we hated the loneliness
and feral anger we shouldered
...because the moon ached to slip
its lacy black dress ...because
can we my tongue begged your breasts
survive our divorces,
resume living without illusions

of fulfillment and your fingers
etched *yes yes of course yes* into
the resistant steel of my back
...because thought reduced to breath
...because your raindrop and hammering kiss
...because your scent ...because pain
is pleasure's most exotic spice
...because the firm dough of your thighs
...because groaning, because such
delicious thrusting ...because along
the trembling fault of our bodies
darkness swallowed grieving
...because forgetting ...because dying
...because please be never-ending
...because somehow I trusted
that you would never hurt me
...O because because release

...because morning, ghosts of heartbreak rising
...because breakfast, shyness ...because coffee
...because our untuned domesticity
...because my familiar robe of silence
...because loss ...because bruising ...because hearts
deafened to promising, hearts too battered
to display their crests of wanting ...because
the sweet, terrible relief of parting
...because alone I crave aimless sailing
...the sky is my bed and I am the air
...breathed in by everyone then exhaled free,
no vows to ensnare, no household to break
...because the wind's hands touch everywhere
yet not even gravity can hold me—
my emptiness refuses sex, deceit,
love, and disappointment with reckless glee

...because my memory contains only
the sound of Ôm ...because, elemental,
I am indifferent to wives, stillness,
lovers, storms ...because, in nothingness,
I am formless perfect infinite free—
pointless without the earth

The Pain of Divorce

is not the same
as cancer killing the body,
though it eats from inside out.

The shock of divorce is not
rockfall flooding the mine shaft
but parting from light and air,
the entombment of love.

If you've sifted through debris
of a tornado-razed home,
you might weep at the random
fury of divorce.

The election rigged,
the town hall fire—
old rotten politics—war,
differ from divorce
overthrowing order.
Though hearts turn lawless,
memory burns.

The loneliness of divorce
is not Sunday, an empty church,
but a saltless Eucharist,
silence of the organ.

The end of divorce
is not sacred rings shelved
like pawn shop junk,
not paperwork, not even
the solar eclipse
of a new lover, but slow

acceptance, hands
warmed by the fire
of happiness in others.

The end of divorce
is the willingness to venture
into the pine-scented night
wine woozy,
humming a distant tune—

I am wounded again
by joy.

My friend, by now you've made your way

to the Pittatore farmhouse,
the grape-stripped hills of Barolo;
you've crossed continents, cultures,
centuries it must seem, to see
our Italian friends—ten years gone—
fatigue of taxis, diesel train,
that damn Satti bus, burning off
faster than *la nebbia*
in summer when the gate opens—
red shingled roof crunch of the white
stone drive Raffaella floating
from the doorframe smiling, unaged,
goose down, sunshine in simple heels.

It's February 26th,
the late afternoon light blinding
off fresh snowfall near Earthquake Park
in Anchorage. My skis skid
to a stop after a short climb,
and, after a year of setbacks,
heart still somehow working, I trick
myself into standing atop
Cannubi hill. I'd forgotten
about your trip. Days? Months since we've
last spoken? You're showing your wife
le Langhe, so reliving first
gelato moans. Lucky bastard.
My stomach growls deep like the earth
insisting the season change Now.
Grissini, porcini, tartufi,
noccioli, agnolotti—
was the language made to sing food?
The hands of the vines wave me in.
I hear them beckon, "Viene qua."

O, how I wish we could stagger
down Via Crosia at dusk
after sampling the barrels
at Sandrone's cantina—
swim the drowsy, crush-flooded air—
school the local kids at Ping-Pong,
sail the market for fresh figs and
le donne…No, no drowning
in nostalgia for me nor
envying your return journey,
and if you think me sentimental
you're wrong—I've lived alone long enough
to learn that thinking of loved ones
is church. It's too easy
to make a worship out of loss,
which is why such gladness lifts me—
to find you near so soon! To rest
briefly not in my Alaskan
home, not even in that enchanting
Italian hamlet, but sated
within the wine-blushed walls
of the four-chambered house of friendship,
which smells nothing like snow, distance,
nothing like white truffles or hurt.

Notes

"Plight Simulator" comes—slightly tweaked and re-cast as a conversation—from lines of computer-generated dialogue printed in the September 2010 issue of *Harper's*.

"The Midday Voice of George Yeats" quotes *Yeats: The Man and the Masks* by Richard Ellman.

"The Door There Is Devastation" takes its title from a line by the Sufi poet Rumi.

"The Muse" appears courtesy of painter Dennis Lind Beery. Please visit www.dennislind.com for more of his fascinating work.

The song "The Book of Love" mentioned in "A Long Way from Cape Town" is a tune by The Magnetic Fields, which I heard performed live by Peter Mulvey and Anaïs Mitchell at the Talkeetna Roadhouse. Thank you Jim Kloss and Esther Golton for hosting an incredible concert at one of the best venues on the planet.

The New York Quarterly Foundation, Inc.
New York, New York

Poetry Magazine
Since 1969

Edgy, fresh, groundbreaking, eclectic—voices from all walks of life.

Definitely NOT your mama's poetry magazine!

The *New York Quarterly* has been defining the term contemporary American poetry since its first craft interview with W. H. Auden.

Interviews • Essays • and of course, lots of poems.

www.nyquarterly.org

No contest! That's correct, NYQ Books are NO CONTEST to other small presses because we do not support ourselves through contests. Our books are carefully selected by invitation only, so you know that NYQ Books are produced with the same editorial integrity as the magazine that has brought you the most eclectic contemporary American poetry since 1969.

Books

nyqbooks.org

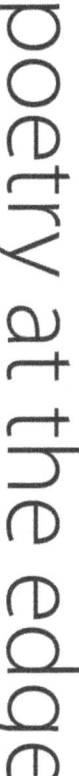

poetry at the edge™

www.ingramcontent.com/pod-product-compliance
Lightning Source LLC
LaVergne TN
LVHW041339080426
835512LV00006B/537